How to Be an Indian in the 21st Century

How to Be an Indian in the 21st Century

(Continuing the Oral Tradition)
Tales of an Iroquois Storyteller

LOUIS V. CLARK III
(Two Shoes)

WISCONSIN HISTORICAL SOCIETY PRESS

Published by the Wisconsin Historical Society Press
Publishers since 1855

The Wisconsin Historical Society helps people connect to the past by collecting,
preserving, and sharing stories. Founded in 1846, the Society is one of the
nation's finest historical institutions.
Order books by phone toll free: (888) 999-1669
Order books online: shop.wisconsinhistory.org
Join the Wisconsin Historical Society: wisconsinhistory.org/membership

Cover art inspired by an illustration by the author.

Printed in the United States of America
Designed by Percolator Graphic Design

21 20 19 18 17 2 3 4 5

Library of Congress Cataloging-in-Publication Data
Names: Clark, Louis V., III, author.
Title: How to be an Indian in the 21st century / Louis V. Clark III (Two Shoes).
Description: Madison : Wisconsin Historical Society Press, [2017]
Identifiers: LCCN 2016034794 (print) | LCCN 2016036065 (e-book) |
 ISBN 9780870208157 (pbk. : alk. paper) | ISBN 9780870208164 (e-book) |
 ISBN 9780870208164 (E-book)
Subjects: LCSH: Clark, Louis V., III. | Clark, Louis V., III—Poetry. | Oneida
 Indians—Wisconsin—Biography. | Oneida Indians—Poetry. | Indians of
 North America—Wisconsin—Biography.
Classification: LCC PS3603.L36526 Z46 2017 (print) | LCC PS3603.L36526 (e-book) |
 DDC 811/.6 [B] —dc23
LC record available at https://lccn.loc.gov/2016034794

To Debra Lee Grace (VanEnkevort) Clark

Contents

Kanuhwelatuksla

Traditional Oneida Thanksgiving Prayer

Now listen to the words that come before all else.

We bring together our minds and give thanks to one another.
So be it our minds.

We bring together our minds and give thanks to our Mother
the Earth, for the life she gives.
So be it our minds.

We bring together our minds and give thanks for the first fruits
that grow, the strawberry.
So be it our minds.

We bring together our minds and give thanks for all the
medicines.
So be it our minds.

We bring together our minds and give thanks to the tobacco
we use to send our messages to the Creator.
So be it our minds.

We bring together our minds and give thanks to all the different
animals that help sustain our lives.
So be it our minds.

We bring together our minds and give thanks to all the different
trees, the maple is the most special of all.
So be it our minds.

We bring together our minds and give thanks to all the waters
great and small.
So be it our minds.

We bring together our minds and give thanks to all the different
 birds that entertain us.
So be it our minds.

We bring together our minds and give thanks to the forces that
 work together with the earth, our Grandfathers the Thunders,
 who bring the rain to renew the earth.
So be it our minds.

We bring together our minds and give thanks to the eldest
 Brother the Sun, who gives us light and warmth.
So be it our minds.

We bring together our minds and give thanks to our Grandmother
 the Moon, she controls all the life cycles on earth.
So be it our minds.

We bring together our minds and give thanks to the stars that are
 our relatives, they beautify the sky.
So be it our minds.

We bring together our minds and give thanks to the four
 messengers who give us guidance.
So be it our minds.

We bring together our minds and give thanks to the Creator of all,
 for it is the Creator who has brought us together as one.
So be it our minds.

I.

My name is Louis Clark.

Louis Vincent Damian Clark III.

They call me Two Shoes.

I am of two worlds.

My Father's People were from Europe, from Poland.

My Mother's People were here waiting for them.

I am one with the People of the Standing Stone.

We are the Oneida Tribe of Indians of Wisconsin.

I am a part of the Iroquois Confederacy, a member of the Bear Clan.

I am guided by the Hawk.

I started to write poetry when I was in the sixth grade.

Sixth-grade boys, who write poetry, on the reservation, inside of a
 Catholic school,

They get beat up a lot!

But there is poetry in the air on the reservation.

It called to me. I can hear it in my head. I can hear it in my heart.

I was schooled in the art of storytelling by my elders.

Through the blue haze of cigarette smoke, around the kitchen table

That served as our campfire, a world was opened to me.

Sometimes from deep inside of a beer bottle, brandy bottle, stark
 truths were shared.

I share them with you.

Understanding that humans are contradictory,

And all good stories are partly truth and partly fiction.

II.

On the Fourth of July in Oneida, in my memories, Indians would gather. Indians from all over would gather at the ball diamond, located just one good baseball throw west of the Holy Apostles Church in Oneida, Wisconsin. Teepees would rise like the phoenix being reborn. Tents, campfires, and logs for sitting could be seen outlining the baseball infield. Gathered around home plate would be the drums. Not the white man drums that you hear on television, *Boom, boom boom boom! Boom, boom boom boom!*

No, these drums were Indian drums beating *boom, boom, boom, boom, boom, boom,* like a heartbeat, the heartbeat of my nation. They beat all day, they beat all night, and to a little Indian boy tucked inside his bed, those drums made him feel secure.

So I wrote:

4th of July in Oneida

Off in the distance
In my memory I hear
The drums, the drums,
The drums drawing near

The heartbeat of my nation
That sounds this time of year
The drums, the drums,
The drums drawing near

White man's Independence Day
Old Glory waving clear
The drums, the drums,
The drums drawing near

Father standing tall and proud
On his breath a trace of beer
The drums, the drums,
The drums drawing near

My future, my past
My hopes and all my fears
The drums, the drums,
The drums drawing near

My wife, my children
My heritage to hold dear
The drums, the drums,
The drums drawing near

In the sixth grade all my poems had the repeating word. Sadly, like my comic books and baseball cards, they were all thrown away. I was born on the Oneida reservation, about five miles west of Green Bay, Wisconsin. It seemed I spent the first four or five years of my life being raised by my Gramma House, in a little shack on the south side of the tracks with no indoor plumbing. So I wrote this poem about my fear of going to the outhouse after dark:

The Outhouse

On the worn path
With the blanket of
Summer to cover us
Mother Nature held
Little boy secrets
As we ran in the night.

Came the snow
That old trickster lady
Betrayed our confidences
Exposing our fears
Along the path
Grandma would tell us
Of her sorrow
Painted in yellow snow.

Sadly, my heritage was almost thrown away. Our reservation was slowly disappearing. My birth brought responsibilities to a youngster not yet home from the hospital. My older brother Daniel, who had died of crib death years earlier, was the firstborn male heir to the Clark name. It would be many granddaughters later before another male Clark entered the world—me. I was given the surname Clark, so for all practical purposes I was white. No one ever told me I was an Indian. The doctor didn't pull the baby out with those salad tongs and holler, "Hey, an Indian." No, this was the 1950s and you really didn't want to be labeled "red." It wasn't until I entered grade school that I discovered I was an Indian, and this is how that happened.

First-Grade Lessons

I was flat on my back, getting hit in the face
When a young man informed me, what was my race.
I was bleeding and crying but I couldn't agree
I didn't look like anything I saw on TV.
I didn't have a pony, I only had a cat
My Daddy didn't wear a loincloth, thank god for that.

I never smoked a peace pipe
Or burned someone at the stake.
I was just a little kid
Oh, for heaven's sake.

We thought that we were people, my relatives and I
Living, breathing human beings until the day we die.
But religion called us savages, heathens if you will
They paint our face as mascots, like animals that you kill.
That's the way it always is
The way it's always been
But what about this Jesus,
What color was his skin?

I always had a problem with Jesus being blue-eyed and blond, as depicted on the holy cards and statues that I saw. I didn't mind blue eyes, I have them, but blond? Only the baby Jesus. I like to think that Jesus could have been an Indian. But I was a savage. Someone the Christians came over to save.

I just wanted to be a normal kid. So I wrote:

Normal Kid

I was just a normal kid, a normal little boy
My Daddy said "my little man," my Momma her pride
 and joy
They said I had the bluest eyes, my skin a beautiful tan
It wasn't until the first grade, I learned I was an Indian.
(Redskin, papoose, chief, you know)

Then all at once it happened, I was doing fine at school
But if you're born an Indian, it really wasn't cool

The teachers always told me that I should do my best
But when I did, the white boys would sit upon my chest.
(Hitting me in the head, beating me up, kids' stuff)

I marched right home to Momma, I marched right home
 to Dad
I asked if being an Indian was really something bad
They looked upon the bruises, covering my face
So Momma called the Principal and put a contract on my
 race.
(I'm sure she didn't mean to, but that's life.)

That's when I started to wonder, what kind of Indian am I
I don't look like a movie one, except for my blue eyes.
I really don't talk funny and my stomach isn't flat
I don't have just one tear in my eye, what kind of Indian
 is that?
(I wasn't born with feathers, either.)

So I asked myself a teacher, I promised him a bribe
I'd teach him all about bingo, if he'd teach me of my tribe.
He said I might be Oneida, or Menominee or Crow
But I said that all the white boys called me "stupid"
Dontcha know.

(Stupid must be a tribal name
At least in Congress wouldn't you think?
When you get older they say
We join a procreating tribe,
F—— Indian,
That's what they yell when they have a drink
Or when they're sober and with friends

Oh, well.)
THE END.

Here's how I think I got blue eyes.

How an Indian Got Blue Eyes

I won't say that my ears were big
When I was a child,
But when my Momma let me out to play
Left me to run wild
My sisters grabbed me by the neck and hauled me to the
 woods
Stuck a feather in my nose and said I really could

They said fly, fly
Fly away, kid

I ran away as fast I could but it wasn't fast enough
They took me to a sand cliff but I thought I'd call their bluff
I took off straight a' running and jumped into the air
And there I was a flying without strings, without a care

They said fly, fly
Fly away, kid

That's where I flew straight down the hill and landed on
 my head
My sisters gathered round me 'cause they thought that I
 was dead
They said they should call my Momma and talk about their
 fears
Landing on my nose like that made it bigger than my ears

They said fly, fly
Fly away, kid

They carried me right home you see and Mother was aghast
She said my first time in the woods would surely be my last
'Cause with two ears like Dumbo and a nose like a kangaroo
The police would take me off the rez and put me in the zoo

They said blue, blue
Black and blue eyes
Blue, blue,
Pretty blue eyes, that's me.

My Mother looked to the white world, where success seemed that it could, by careful planning and diligent work, be gained and measured. She sought education far from the reservation, leaving to rent herself out as a domestic of sorts to earn room and board while attending high school. She did many things, accomplished many things, while the men were off fighting World War II.

She received an award from Eleanor Roosevelt for a drawing that she did.

She played baseball on traveling teams across the Midwest.

She was a left-handed-hitting, right-handed-throwing out-fielder.

Then the boys came home. She was pushed to the back of the bus and began to disappear.

So I wrote:

1944

I wish that I would have known you
Back in 1944
When dreams lay all before you
Life was knocking at your door
When mundane moments of memory
Were orchids bursting into bloom
I wish that I would have known you
But glory fades too soon

I saw your pretty picture
I heard the many stories
Vested fully in your prime
You reached for greater glory
Eleanor came from Washington
To acknowledge your talent in art
And baseball, like "a league of your own"
Earned a place within my heart

Your beauty was more than youth
With your cat-like eyes of grey
Child-like innocence filled your soul
When you led your children to pray
Once upon a time
Before dreams crashed to the floor
I wish that I would have known you
Back in 1944.

My Father, after fighting in World War II and Korea, looked to the Indian way of life. He said, after being all over the world, that the white world made up only about 10 percent of the population. He

said that life in the circle seemed better than life on a linear plane. He also said that if your belly is full, and you are warm, everything else is a bonus. Little boys don't always understand.

Poppa

Poppa,
Oh Poppa
I remember
 your tattooed arm
With Mother's name
 written green
In the skin
 wrapped around my chest.

Timing my breathing to yours
So the beer in your belly
Wouldn't nauseate me
As you blew it upon me.
I dreamt of escape

Counting your fingers
 like a convict
Counts the bars
 of his cell
Waiting for the time
 my sentence
Would end.

I struggled against
The warmth
 you tried

To show me
 in love.

We all have guilt. Somewhere, somehow, secrets.

Momma Cried

Momma cried alone in the night
Like a burglar stealing jewels
She stole moments to be human
Yet, come the morning, she regressed
This she tried to hide
By anointing herself
With cold water.

Momma cried alone in the house
With Poppa packed off to work
Children bused off to school
Moisture that formed on the glass
Was only the reflection of her
Tumbling, rolling, spilling
On the table
Mixing with yesterday
A bad dream
Dreamt each night.

Momma cried alone on the couch
Her half-baked dinner on the stove
Waiting until she pulled herself
Together—or for the children
To fix, to feed Poppa

A story, a line, a lie
Momma's sick again.

We all became Momma
Trapped by an orange juice
Tomato juice container
That no one else could drink
Trapped
By a lie we all lived
We all told
We all sang
To our friends
To Family
To ourselves.

I saw my friends suffer, too. So I wrote "Morning after Friday."

Morning after Friday

No muffled sounds of love
Ever echoed through the hallways
Of the housing project that I knew.

Multistoried brick buildings
Cast shadows of Teepees—Longhouses
In a forest void of mighty pines.

A child was heard sobbing, praying
On concrete porch steps with the sun
Weeping golden rays upon his back.

An older child peels an orange
With his teeth grimacing
The acid taste drips upon his tongue.

Together the children race to the woods
Grasping homemade bows—arrows
To play what their parents had forgotten.

Shooting, maiming empty cans of beer
A finger dipped in victim's blood
Touched lips, the enemy, a war.

And the final insult to this creature we call humanity, "Closed
Eyes":

Closed Eyes

When Momma beat my Daddy and my Daddy beat my Mom
The sun kept right on shining, no one said that it was wrong
The only consequences that we came to know
Was an eerie silence in the house we kids were left alone.

Sometimes there'd be extra treats, a pizza pie or chips
Sometimes there'd be motel rooms they called "the special
 trips"
Sometimes there'd be extra cash to buy a comic book
Always there were sunglasses to hide that certain look.

Some days the air hung heavy like God had gone away
Little boys just held their breath, too afraid to pray
Nighttime fell upon us, hopes of dreamless sleep
Curse of morning woke us up, we lost our soul to keep.

My sisters said adoption, which meant I didn't belong
Another form of refuge, for me a freedom song
Many countless hours trying to fit in
Where is life enchanted, where do we begin?

Is life out there for all of us or are windows always shaded?
Is Superman an Indian or are his ethics faded?
We share his dual personality, secrets we can't share
We hide our grim realities for no one seems to care.

There are many problems on and off the reservation, as I knew living in a white/Indian home. To top it off, I was Catholic, too. This put a bit of a strain on my life—not only was I a member of the heathen, savage race that Christians came to America to save, but it wasn't until the late 1960s that I, as a Catholic, was allowed to ride the bus. Which made me eligible for a whole new set of rules and encounters, for which I wrote:

Rules

Thursday is Queers Day, that's what we always heard
If you wear a yellow shirt, you're considered weird
I had the nicest yellow shirt that Momma made me wear
The kids all said that I was queer, Momma didn't seem to
 care
I didn't know just what it was,
This thing called queer, you see
But I heard them laughing
and they all laughed at me

The girls they had them cooties
So we kept our fingers crossed

The playground had Cowboys and Indians
You know who always lost
To top it off of all the things
I was Polish, too
Momma said ignore those kids
Dad said POW!
Punch them in the kazoo

Momma's way was peaceful
Though I cried at night
Daddy's way was different
Standing up for what was right
But was it right to fight each day
'Cause fighting never ends
And if you're always fighting folks
You're never making friends

Again
What was a cootie
Or a queer
They never did tell
But life upon the playground
Can be a living hell

This all happened only if I survived the bus ride to school.

Red Muse

"You're in my seat" he said to me
I looked around, I could see
Plenty of spots on that old bus
Where we could sit, the two of us

"You're in my seat" he said to me
Then slapped my head repeatedly
'Til tears were streaming down my face
Swallowing my pride I moved my place

Deep in the bowels of the library
Edgar Rice Burroughs and history
Told of a group, Neanderthal man
Descended from apes, not Tarzan
My fears came true each afternoon
No boy, no man, but one big baboon

"You're in my seat" he'd say each day
And slapped me hard as I slunk away
Attempting to talk to change his mind
He slapped me again time after time
'Til one day I stood my ground
I stood tall I wouldn't back down
He hit me again but I was right
So I hit him hard with all my might

In libraries are written stories
Of brave young men and all their glories
I was standing eye to eye
I knew in my heart I was gonna die
Yet I stood facing my fear
Though doom lay ahead abundantly clear

"You're in my seat" he laughed at me
Then moved me toward a wounded knee
With kicks and blows to my integrity
"You're in my seat" he laughed at me

I stood up, I'll stand again
But I stood alone, where are my friends?

My friends were just as frightened as I was. Sometimes you just have to stand up for yourself.

Wounded Knee was considered the last battle of the Indian Wars. But it was no battle.

Battle of Wounded Knee

What was the last
On an admissions test
They asked
Battle of the Indian wars

At a hallowed place to learn
Where all lying
Should be spurned
Truth, justice should open every door

Leave it to our son
To take the test
And run
The battle was no battle in the snow

The 7th Cavalry
Shot each Indian
Attempting to flee
Medals of Honor we call Murderers Row

Fifteen Indian guns were shown
Left on a pile
But one unknown
Shot rang out to start a bloody mess

With the cavalry surround
They shot, they shot each other
Down
With friendly fire from four cannons I confess

They called it victory
It was murder
Plain you see
History calls it Battle when Indians died
And the 7th Cavalry
Written as heroes
In history
Sang this little ditty on their ride

300 little Indians around, 300 little Indians
Shoot one down into the ground, 299 Little Indians around
 299 Little Indians around, 299 little Indians Shoot one
 down into the ground 298 little Indians around . . .

Then I was bused off the reservation to attend high school. Here I
was to learn about the doctrine of "Cooperate and Graduate." I was
informed that I did not have to study or do homework to graduate.
All I had to do was keep my mouth shut and stay out of trouble.
Keeping my mouth shut and staying out of trouble was difficult,
to say the least. Yet out of these experiences were born two poems.

White Man

I'm what you call a white man from my head down to my toes.
I get up in the morning and I put on white man's clothes
I drink the white man's coffee, I watch the white man's shows
That's why I am a white man as everybody knows.

I was born in a white man's hospital around 1958
I suckled on a rubber nipple that I learned to hate
They sent me to the Catholic school where I learned to pray
 That I wouldn't get beaten up nearly every single day
Then it was to high school where it was my fate
 To never learn to study, just cooperate
I often think about the things that I might have learned
The school got their tax money and all I got was burned.

Thanks to Affirmative Action I could get any janitor's work
Wear my Daddy's hand-me-downs, a nice blue-collar shirt
Found my ladder to success but every rung was broke
Equal opportunity, another white man's joke
There's a thing called introspection that could be just a curse
Could it be my personality that just makes things go worse
Maybe it's the way I am and really not my race
I seem to do all right they say when I know my place

I let the injun jokes I hear slip right on through my ears
Can't waste my time a' worrying about ungrounded fears
Management can lie to you or speak their racial minds
Nothing is illegal except during a specific time
Nothing in here is racial, it's just anti-you
But if it's anti-me it's an Indian who gets screwed
Earn your way the old-fashioned way really is a game
The only problem that I see I was born with the wrong name

I'm what you call a white man from my head down to my toes.
I get up in the morning and I put on white man's clothes
I drink the white man's coffee, I watch the white man's shows
That's why I am a white man as everybody knows.
I guess I'll never really win, I guess I'll always lose

It's just that I have darker skin I never got to choose
They just can't see beyond some things they won't give me a
 chance
They live their lives in rainstorms 'cause they make me dance
But liberty and justice are still worth fighting for
Praying that my children will find the open doors
All I know of living is what I hope to be
Only when we all go blind will everybody see.

I'm what you call Oneida, wearing white man's clothes
But folks call me an Indian because of white man's shows
I've withstood all the bigotry, I've shouldered all the blows
I'm what you call Oneida from my head down to my toes.

Many of us, throughout the years, were taken off the reservation
to learn to become white. We were sent to schools. Two things I
never could quite understand were circumcisions and proctolo-
gists. This misunderstanding led to another poem, with the caveat
that little boys like to write their names in the snow.

The Legend of Acorn
The Only Circumcised Indian on the Reservation

Hey look to the horizon
And see what I can see
Reservation boy surprising
Who they called Acorn when he'd pee
His Daddy was a white man
His Momma proper and prim
She didn't know about the hospitals
And all the things they'd trim

Acorn
They called him Acorn.
He never was the same
Especially when writing names
Acorn
They called him Acorn
But he said that it's all right
This proves that I am white

His Mother shed a little tear
When she saw what they had done
Where he was a little boy
He now had almost none.
And they call us savages
We should stay where we belong
But what they do to babies
You know it must be wrong

Acorn
They called him Acorn.

He lived his life by the golden rule
And then was sent to Catholic school
Where the teacher finally said
Your skin is really, really red
He said that I can prove I'm white
I'll do it now if it's all right
She said she'd give him just one chance
So he turned around and dropped his pants

Acorn
They called him Acorn.

The nuns they beat him with a stick
And when he'd taken every lick
They banished him to the great unknown
Public school far away from home
They enrolled him in his first gym class
Where you had to shower in bare "mmm"
And he was surely shocked to see
He said, "Everyone is carved like me"

Acorn
They called him Acorn.

Then on graduation day
He got a job to earn his pay
First on to the Doctor sent
To gnash his teeth his clothes to rent
The Doctor put a rubber glove on
And after that Acorn was gone.
He said that you can tell the Prez
They never do that on any rez
First they cut you when you're little
Then they poke you when you're tall
I don't want to be a white man
A white man at all!!!

However, high school did have its rewards. I learned that to sur-
vive, I had to be a "crazy Indian." Not always fun, not always
wise, but in the long run it saved me from being picked on. More
than forty years later I was told that I was respected by the other
Indian kids at the school because I never was picked on. On the
other hand I spent many an hour sitting by myself in the office. I
deserved it, but I didn't get beat up much anymore.

All I had were sisters
My Daddy loved John Wayne
So for my misconceptions
I'm really not to blame?

Saturday's Hero

Saturday on the town
Greeting each beer
Like a long-lost love
Pressing her to my lips
Drain her of all her passions
To feel them cycle
Through my veins.

How many we never counted
Until we counted our wallets empty
They just slid inside
Gathering, waiting
Like a mob
Until in strength they spoke
Mindless words.

A fist can fly
Kiss my head
Skin to skin
Blood to blood
The floor would catch me
Throwing me back to my feet.

When blood started to warm
Like a liquid heating pad

The alcohol inside
Would save me from all pain.

I'd lash out and hot damn
If John Wayne himself
Wouldn't stand behind me
Guiding my fists
And as I struck
And as I was struck
I couldn't help but think
"When's the commercial."

The best thing that ever happened to me, however, did happen in high school. I saw this young lady, blue blouse, blue skirt, high heels, and the biggest smile on her face as she was walking down the hallway. So naturally, after building up the courage, I asked her to go out with me. Not only did this young lady have looks, charm, and grace, she also had intellect and she politely turned me down. I'm nothing else if not persistent, so after a year of me asking her out, her mother and older sister made her go out with me. I've written many poems for her in our more than forty years together.

Dancing with the Phone

Passions
New passions
Discovered only in love's
Aging process
Turning hours
To minutes
To seconds
At a glance

Sweet sixteen
Shadows
Loves speak
Across the years
Across the kitchen floor
Dancing with the phone cord
At a glance.

Sitting
Weary in my years
Watching
Smiling with
A Grandmother who
Shares my bed
Sweet sixteen
At a glance

Staring
Passions build
She glides
She floats
Dancing with the phone
Sweet sixteen
Forever
At a glance.

And:

Sea of Yellow

Planted in a garden
Of innocence and surprise

Blooming in virgin soil
Right before my eyes
Dreams I never dared
Hopes I never dreamed
Dancing slowly in the night
A soft romantic scene
Played before an audience
For forty years each day
Love becomes a sculptress
Molding us like clay
'Til in our years our innocence
Sipping just like wine
In my child-like love for you
I give a dandy lion.

We joined our forces together and looked seven generations ahead. To plant the seeds for our family's growth, we had to run away to become only us. And education, as my Mother had seen, led the way.

I started college, and twenty-five years later I graduated. During these years, we enjoyed a lifetime of experiences. Working during the day and going to school at night, sometimes I indulged my passions and studied poetry. Here I learned that as a poet, I was willing to show the world who Louis Clark truly was, and my first success was a poem called "A Scalp for the Indian."

The Oneidas were farmers. My mother and father were both raised on farms, and we had a small farm as I was growing up. From time to time we raised horses, cows, chickens, pigs, sheep, and rabbits. We also had a monstrous garden filled with many taste-tempting vegetables.

I was the head rock picker. One day as I was picking rocks in the spring and my father was plowing, he asked if I wanted to plow. There I was in my white T-shirt, sleeves appropriately rolled up just a bit, blue jeans with a cuff, and my work boots on. I was an Indian James Dean riding that old tractor. I had my diesel wound up and the smoke was blowing black as coal, as the song "Six Days on the Road" played in my head.

Unfortunately, we had the same type of tractor as a neighbor who had met his demise a few years earlier by flipping the tractor over and upon himself. You put the plow in a bit too low, add just a little too much speed, and the front end of this tractor comes off the ground. Well, my mother saw me, and as I said before, my brother was already dead, and so there I was picking rocks, once again.

This time while picking rocks, I found a small iron hoe head. My Father did some research, probably starting at the White Eagle Tavern, and eventually he discovered just what we had found. This little hoe head was one of the first items the French traders had traded with the Indians. It was used for scraping hides, but he surmised that after a while it was a great weapon for revenge.

According to my Father, the settlers in New England had paid for Indians to be eliminated. In 1653 the New England Trading Company put out a bounty on Indians, and the evidence that needed to be produced to prove an Indian had died was a scalp bearing red skin. Thus, the term redskin is quite offensive to my People.

My Father also showed that television was wrong even in the way it showed scalping. The little hoe we had found was the perfect weapon. One would kneel behind the victim, cradling the

victim's head between the legs. Pulling back on the hair of the scalp, one would slowly and methodically peel the skin away from the body. So I wrote my first publishable poem.

A Scalp for the Indian

The first cut filled his lap
Dripping and spilling
Like a fresh, lanced boil
The second splattered his face
Marking him with the pox
Of greed and revenge
The third shorter, cleaner
More like peeling wax
From a silver candle holder
Was the correct stroke
Cutting, peeling
Chopping, peeling
He finished
Holding his lesson high
Veins formed upon the
Outside of his skin
Down his arms
Over his chest
Like acid rain.

Hurled into the fire
The lesson burned white
Burned black in sin
A smelting hearth
Imploding English shadows

Exploding into new myths
Only the fine lines
That speed readers miss
Would remember his brothers
His sisters and the bounty
Today the farmer's plow
unearths the iron hoe.

At this time, I also felt the need to exorcise the demons that had haunted me since my sister had died at twenty-one years of age while I was only fourteen. At fourteen, one looks only at oneself.

Grieve Not for the Dead

I saw you lie
Upon a bed of innocence
Your half brain swollen
Like a balloon bursting
Your neck painted red
Your veins spit out
What they tried to feed you.

Yesterday, sister, a child
Standing on the sidewalk
 kicking strangers
Creating an impression
Strong willed
A mustang running free.

Today, a dove
Rare, gentle, free
Lit upon alfalfa fields

Stealing beauty
From each new blossom.

Now we stand
Hands folded, pretending
Your bed is not a casket
Telling lies
To a pair of eyes
That know
We are fools.

When a memory
I'll wish that I had held you
In my arms like the child
And told the truth
To the woman
If it were me
Or I was you
A part of me is.

III.

My dream was to write, my reality was to live. My wife and I, along with our family, farmed on a small scale. We were on the church board, we taught religion, we volunteered at other programs, and we formed the first baseball association in our city. I coached or helped coach youth baseball for nineteen years. I also helped coach some basketball, and we have some very embarrassing pictures of me in my coaching shorts. From my interaction with the players, I discovered that many parents wished for success more than the players did themselves.

So I wrote:

Superstar

No I'm not a candidate, no headlines will be mine
My pedigree excluded me, my star has yet to shine
I do ok at baseball games, can't hit or run or catch
I sit the bench and play right field when they toss the ball
 I fetch

They signed me up for football too, they thought I'd be a star
But getting hit and hitting back, no way that I'd go far
Then wrestling and soccer came, it's more than I can take
Don't they know my brittle bones are often prone to break

Then Tiger Woods he made it big so Dad bought me some
 clubs
But golfing too was not my thing, at that I was a dud
Basketball in my underwear, I guess that I did fine
Couldn't shoot or dribble or set a pick but was good at riding
 pines

My poor old Dad would get so mad, I never seemed to play
My Mother too she never knew, to sit the bench I prayed
I don't know when it all began, it's hidden in our history
To be a jock would be a shock for me, a real mystery

I like to run, it's kinda fun,
But I really hate to fight
If all I did was be a kid
To me it'd be all right.

Then for fun:

Little League Pitcher

I'm the greatest little league pitcher
Of that there is no doubt
I've never had a batter
Who could ever hit one out
Though I never throw no-hitters
It's just not what I do
I lay the ball in easy
They hit it where I want them to.

I'm the greatest little league pitcher
Of that there is no doubt
My fastball is like lightning
My change-up like a draught
I never throw a curveball
I don't think that it's a charm
And very few pro players
Make it with just one arm.

I'm the greatest little league pitcher
Of that there is no doubt
If a batter acts like Babe Ruth
I simply strike them out
But if I see the batter
Really has no chance
I throw the ball and hit the bat
And watch the runner dance.

I'm the greatest little league pitcher
Of that there is no doubt
Whenever I walk out on the field
My family stands to shout
They think it's really pretty cool
They think it's kind of nifty
To see their Dad in little league
Although he's over fifty.

> Signed
> The Coach

Along the way, the white and red flowing inside of my veins did boil to the point of causing problems from time to time. No matter how we face it, we always run into racism. This is how I earned my name "Two Shoes," simply because I was afraid to do anything wrong and jeopardize what I had.

Two Shoes

They call me Two Shoes
As in "goody"
Trained to toe the line

Two Shoes, as in "goody"
Afraid to speak my mind.

A fist came flying from the night to change my point of view
A bottle poured inside my home poisoned my parents too
Watched my sisters state their cause and the havoc that ensued
Even parties I always feared for the trouble that they brewed

Two Shoes as in "goody"

Catholic nuns in their black and white world taught me all
 about sin
Noble blood coursing through my veins a game I couldn't win
Columbus came to save my soul no thoughts of what might
 have been
My ancestors, pagan trash, in heaven they couldn't get in.

Survived my grades, survived my class, even survived their praise
That pierced my heart, scarred my soul, in search of better days
Bit my tongue, shield my eyes, from unforgiving gaze
When in doubt side with might it's me, (the loser) who always
 pays.

Two Shoes, as in "goody"
Trained to toe the line
Two Shoes as in "goody"
Afraid to speak my mind.

Edgar Poe, Jerry Jeff, Kris taught me how to drink
Lived my life just out of step, even wore shirts of pink
Could lash out at injustice though, unfazed I didn't blink
But all I got from alcohol was an excuse not to think.

But Arthur, Dante, and Quixote, too, found me at age ten
Allowed me to escape the world when storm clouds came again
Then somehow blest along the line I found a lifelong friend
To stand by me as I found my voice inside this simple pen.

Two Shoes as in "goody"
Trained for all to see
Two Shoes as in "goody"
Let my voice run free.

But my voice wasn't always allowed to run free.

One Dead Indian

There's an aloneness, a feeling
of despair that creeps over me
like a shroud being sewn over
a corpse. It grips my shoulders,
squeezing my chest until there
is a real pain deep down inside
where my heart, my soul resides. Belongs.

And it's a curious occurrence
in that it always occurs when I'm
with people. Deep within the midst of
brothers or mates, that I'm
supposed to be one with. One in
a common goal. United together
for the common good.

It happened again today. And I wouldn't
believe it if you told me about it. I
can't believe it now. But it was there like
a drop of blood on a clean white
sheet.

I was assigned to a crew,
a bridge cleaning crew. Working
State-owned bridges to remove the salt,
the grime from the winter
season. Getting everything ready
for the summer boating season.

I asked the foreman if
he was certified in CPR
emergency operations for
confined space work he said
yes he was but
should anything happen
"You're just one dead Indian."

I dreamed of advancement, for me and my family. There was a
foreman's position offered, and management said that whoever
scored the highest on the test would get the job. After the test it
was announced that there would be interviews and the leading
candidate called me a "damn Indian," among other things. Then
another foreman told me that it wasn't me, it was just my race.

Just Your Race

A Black Cat crossed the road today,
So I pulled on over and said "headin' my way"

He jumped in said he had an ear to share.
So we rode on down to highway one
We rode all day till the day was done
But I left that cat alone and standing there.
'Cause he said:
We may share some moments
But you you're not my kind
When it's just the two of us
Your company's just fine
But when we're out in public
You have to know your place
It's really not you my friend
It's just your race.

Well that's the way my life goes
Never an easy row to hoe
And never a time it seems that I can rest.
Like the time that my old company
Put a promotion before my friend and me
Said we'll give the job to who scores highest on the test.
My friend had trained for a year or so
But his test came back oh so low
Or so it seems 'cause they threw that test away.
They said they'd have an interview
And it came down to just we two
But he said "Indians gonna lose today."
'Cause,
We may share some moments
But you you're not my kind
When it's just the two of us
Your company's just fine

But when we're out in public
You have to know your place
It's really not you my friend
It's just your race.

Well there wasn't much that I could do
I could whine and pout and cry and brood
As I watched the white man bringing home big cash.
But he got fat in his office chair
Lost his pride, his respect, his hair
When he took his honor and threw it in the trash.
The one thing 'bout white society
That separates him from me
Is where we stand when trucking the long haul.
I may be beaten battered down
Have my face pushed deep in the ground
Though I stumble you can bet I never crawl
When they say,
We may share some moments
But you you're not my kind
When it's just the two of us
Your company's just fine
But when we're out in public
You have to know your place
It's really not you my friend
It's just your race.

I just kept on keeping on. Applying and taking tests. I scored the
highest but the next time they went with seniority. Why have the
test?

Racism on the Job

In my dreams
I am a coward

In my dreams
I cry tears of shame

In my dreams
fear flows from my soul
like water from a tap

In my dreams
I am paralyzed
Inept
 unable to respond

Was I dreaming
Today
Too many days

When bullies rent
The fabric of my being

I swallow the bitter herbs
The bitter words
Spat upon my soul

Am I a coward?

When I squash my anger

Rendered a eunuch
By society

Protecting those I love
Trading pride
For honor.

And then you become a little paranoid.

Paranoid

I don't like sounding paranoid, though it happens time and time
 again,
Someone I've built a relationship with, consider them a friend,
Will meet me at a gathering, as they quietly have a drink,
Brain goes in neutral,
Mouth goes in gear,
They speak before they think.

White girls who marry Indians, aren't their morals kind of loose?
Given that you can hunt anytime, you should use a hickory bow
 or spruce.
The way that you waste walleye is a sin against your god.
"I don't hunt, I don't fish" so that opinion's kind of odd.

Living in this land of the free it really is a shame,
That my fists are aching to be used to protect my good wife's
 name,
If my friends can think these thoughts, what about folks that
 I don't know
So this land ain't really free, there's places I can't go.

You don't pay any taxes, so you all have lots of dough
I drove through the reservation, where does your money go?

You live like third world refugees, you really have no class
Bingo bucks and welfare checks, all you do is sit upon your a——.

I really can't respond to them, they think I'm on the dole
I think that they should wear a sign, "add booze for instant
 a——hole."
I guess that it's my frustration, there's little I can do,
They say, "We mean other Indians, we're not talking about you."

A blue-collar life, when college is free, means you must be a loser,
The law's on your side so you must not try, by law they have to
 choose ya.
Yet, any old day you check old N.A. means Not Applicable you see,
They want my experience, knowledge and skills, thing is, they
 don't want me.

Part of the problem I find I have is the shroud I use to survive
I have to make fun, stupid old jokes, to stay sane and keep me
 alive.
I'm never secure; your drinking beer brings forth ignorance
 and hate
Sober old skins never can win, I guess you call it fate.

We honor you going woo, woo, woo, woo, dancing a crazy old
 dance
You say, "I can't win but I love the Redskins, remember you
 didn't give Custer a chance."
Chief Wahoo's teeth, his crazy big nose, the Braves have the
 Tomahawk chop,
I'm fat and I'm lazy, going quite crazy,
Screaming when will it stop!
Praying when will it stop!

Then I thought about the tears of a clown.

Pagliacci Must Have Been Indian

Injuns are Funny.

Told my sister
I wanted to be a cowboy
She laughed at me.

Told my teacher
Wanted to go to college
He laughed at me

Attempted to disappear
Off rez high school
Kids laughed at me.

Twenty-five years of night school
Oh Lordy, cum laude
Peers laughed at me.

Came the big promotion
I had the highest test
Management laughed at me.

I tell you now your mascot
Causes pain to me and mine
The government laughs at me.

Injuns are Funny.

Finally, I had the highest test score to go along with the highest seniority. Still, I was taken alone—this is crucial, as I've come to learn—I was taken alone into the boss's office. Here I was told that

while I had the highest test score and most seniority, they wanted to give the job to someone else. Who just happened to have the last name as another boss. Then I discovered why I always was talked to alone, that way they could say they never said what they said.

Stonewalker

You spit into my face each day
You treat me like a child
Lording out permission
Like a king can drive men wild
It doesn't matter where or when
You've authority to hold
Good leaders are true servants
Or haven't you been told
The Indians had their way, you see
They knew the place and time
All I ever hear from you
Is "What you got, is mine."
They give the civil service tests
But it's really just a game
Bent and molded as you please
The power is in your name.
Laws they pass in Washington
Are laughed at behind closed doors
We have to prove specific points
To judges old and bored
They try the cases with blinders on
You win, we lose, no tie
All you ever have to do
Is smile when you lie.

Yet, growing up amid the vice of alcoholism was good training for encountering racism on the job site. The way it is doled out and the abuses one encounters make it easier to close one eye and attempt to make it a better world. Starting with yourself and then hopefully the people that surround you.

I knew I was different. Perhaps it was my being an Indian, perhaps it is because I'm a poet. I see into tomorrow and hope for a better day. But I was told my poems aren't poems if they rhyme. If one wants to write rhyming poems, head to Nashville (which really wasn't a viable option for an Indian, heading to cowboy country).

Because of the drums pounding in my brain, in my soul, I had to write my poetry in cadence. It just turned out that rhyming was the most fun. I decided to give up my dreams of being a great poet, and I decided to just write what felt good to me.

I also decided to share my work with my crew, now that I was a foreman assigned to drainage chores. We dig ditches and install culverts under state, county, and municipal roads, as well as driveways. We, my crew, take pride in our work, so we attach a poem, in a sealed plastic bag, to each of the culverts we install. On each poem is each crew member's name and responsibility. Maybe, in 50 to 100 years, someone will dig up our culverts and know who we were.

One day at work, I observed in a field what appeared to be a drunken cow. I wrote "Drunken Cow," which is my crew's favorite poem.

Drunken Cow

I went down to the canning factory
Sitting on the edge of town

Where they pick up all the corn
And sell it all year round.
They tear off the stalks, the leaves, and the cobs
Then throw that all away
So the farmers come and pick it up
And feed it just like hay.

Drunken Cow.

It sits there in the noonday sun
Until it's raw and ripe
I never smelled anything that bad
Not even pickled tripe.
Still the farmers go and gather it in
On the checkbook it makes no dent.
They stuff it in a storage bin
And leave it to ferment.

Drunken Cow.

Now cats and rats and mice and dogs
They won't touch them a drop
But to Bessy and Bossy and all their friends
It's become their favorite crop.
They gather together underneath a tree
And munch it all the day.
I do believe it's a coming trend
For a cow to join AA.

Drunken Cow.

I feed it to my cows and then
They grin from ear to ear.

They stagger round and some fall down
Upon their derriere.
I tell you this it ain't no joke
Though some call it a spoof
I put up with these crazy cows
'Cause their milk is 90 proof.

Drunken Cow.

Generally I end this poem here but, if you enjoy a little "rap" beat, I add this last verse.

Drunken cow I don't know how
I'm gonna get you in the barn
But I swear to you and you know it's true
I'll do you all no harm
It's not your meat that tastes so sweet
It's the milk sitting in the pail
I'll live my life with a happy wife
Sipping a Guernsey cocktail.

My crew's next favorite poem was born after a day of facing more than the usual amount of BS. One of the crew members ordered pizza, and the idea for this poem was born when the delivery vehicle arrived, prominently displaying the Italian flag. I started contemplating my great-great-great-great-grandfather sitting on the edge of the Atlantic Ocean. How did he know it was the Atlantic Ocean when he saw the *Nina*, *Pinta*, and the *Santa Maria* floating along, flying the Italian flag? He turned and looked at my great-great-great-great-grandmother and said, "Hey, who ordered pizza?"

Now I full well know that Columbus sailed from Spain. But as I said, I was contemplating stereotypes. I've watched enough Mafia movies to assume that Columbus crossed up the queen and raised the Italian flag just out of sight. Then I flew through scalping and into William Clark, of the Lewis and Clark expedition, and how he served under Andrew Jackson. Which led to my crew's second-favorite poem.

Who Ordered Pizza

I knew a man Columbo,
Not the TV star,
Who got three ships from Spain
'Cause he didn't have a car.
Now Spain expelled the Jews
Back in 1492
And Columbo found the Redman
Now we sing the blues.

Hey, who ordered pizza
I see red, white, and green,
Italian flags upon the ocean
Ain't that what those colors mean.

New England had a trading company
They paid for "injun" scalps.
They blamed it on the Redman
Hey thanks, we didn't need the help.
Seems our daily double
Is getting in lots of trouble
"Injun's" ain't like on TV
Hate to burst your bubble.

Hey, who ordered pizza
And me I got no bread
Think they're willing to barter
And take my land instead?

So manifest your destiny
With William Clark in tow
Andy Jackson snubbed the courts
And raked in lots of dough.
He said let's kill the Redman
And take away his land
There's property in the Bighorn
Ripe for a Custer stand.

Hey, who ordered pizza
I see red, white, and green,
Italian flags upon the ocean
Ain't that what those colors mean.
Hey, who ordered pizza
And me I got no bread
Think they're willing to barter
And take my land instead?
Hey, who ordered pizza.

I was lucky that the men on my crew accepted my work in writing.
I work with some really good men. Most of them supported my
dreams of education, and the dreams for my family.

Coming from the reservation, we wanted our children to have
an education for a chance at a better life. Who knew what doors
could be opened and what opportunities could present themselves
through a dedication to study? I failed to learn this lesson in high

school, and it was only through the school of hard knocks that my eyes were opened.

Our oldest child was recruited by many good schools in the Midwest. He was a top-ten student aided by a 48 percent accuracy from the three-point line on the basketball court. Lawrence University of Appleton came calling. It is a good school, it was close to home, and we came to learn that five of the original thirty-eight students enrolled there were from Oneida—so it was also tradition.

Rik Warch, the Lawrence president, made our family feel at home. In 1997 he spotted our fourth child reading Tennyson, Lord Alfred Tennyson, during halftime of a basketball game. Mr. Warch inquired as to why one would read Tennyson during a basketball game. For enjoyment was the answer. Mr. Warch extended an invitation to attend Lawrence, too, after the completion of high school; there was no need to even apply—acceptance was guaranteed.

I bow to this child's superior knowledge and understanding of poetry as a form of expression. I should like to include his favorite poem, "Men of Honor," a poem about two professional men who were never hesitant to share their knowledge, their professionalism, with me. And here's to our six children, who have all attained their college degrees: Louie, Dawn, Renee, Jacob, Jordan, and Philip.

Men of Honor

Standing there with balding heads
bearded chins of white
Easter Island pillars
holding secrets, edge of night
laden with experience

but not with Stonehenge age
disappear a little each day
youth and impatience turn the page
reveling in arrogant strength
life becomes a mystery
all the knowledge deemed to share
is lost as ancient history.

Standing there with balding heads
bearded chins of white
earning their fate within the sun
sometimes wrong, or right
men I knew years ago
accepting what they'd give
hoping that within this poem
their stories still will live.

IV.

A few years later, it was fall, leaves falling down, squirrels getting ready for the winter, and deer looking for mates. It was hunting season. I found a small ad in the newspaper calling for poetry submissions. The deadline was something like December 1.

Now, during deer season, my family calls me "Dammit missed again," as I'm out there attempting to fill the freezer. Along with knowing that real poems don't rhyme but mine do, I was hesitant. Yet, ask my wife, I'm persistent if nothing else. So I typed up five of my best, or least worst, and on my way to the meat market to purchase food for the freezer on December 1, I mailed in my submissions.

A bit later I received a letter requesting five more poems. They didn't ask for money, so I thought, "Great." Shortly thereafter came a request for thirty-five to forty poems. Still no request for money. Well, that type of work required quite a lot from my two pointer fingers. Each of my family members offered to type up the poems for me, but as any poet knows, poems are living things and can, as well as should, be changed from time to time. A poet works alone. I did it!

Then, a phone call. A Mr. James Parins from the University of Arkansas wanted to let me know that his group enjoyed my poetry and was offering to publish a chapbook for me. And still they were requesting no money. What's the catch? In return all they asked was for me to go out into the world and share my poetry.

(Speeding ahead a bit, I was working as a greeter at a literary conference, the Oshkosh, Wisconsin, Lakefly Literary Conference, when the organizer rushed in, all aflutter, explaining that one of the main speakers had left. Then she looked at me and said, "Can you talk for an hour?" Well, church bells tolled, the 1812 Overture echoed through the halls: certainly I can talk for an hour. It takes

me twenty minutes to say hello. Give me a beer and I can do a whole evening.)

But this was in the beginning.

We heard of a poet society meeting in Appleton, Wisconsin, at the Harmony Café on the third Monday of the month. So we went. My turn came, and tentatively I rose to share my two poems. In the audience were many different types of souls. There was a Cowboy, I was an Indian, there were young people and old people, there were long hairs and short hairs, ponytails and spikes, tattoos and makeup, and they were all looking at me! They were all poets, many were quite successful with books of their own. I read one of the books, in which the poet dreamed of killing her husband. I was scared.

After I finished my reading, the first person who came to me, requesting to buy a book, which I didn't have, was the Cowboy. Wasn't that something!

Cowboys and Indians

Beer and Pretzels

Love and marriage

Cheese and sausage

Babies and diapers

Chips and salsa

Mamas and Daddies

Ketchup and mustard

Pickles and onions

The Lone Ranger and Tonto

Tonto and the Lone Ranger

Batman and Robin

The Green Hornet and Kato

Simon and Garfunkel

 Sonny and Cher

Nadia Comaneci and Bela Karolyi
I can do it on my own
So can I

I'm an Indian

A warrior

Stoic.

Reading Poetry

 Reading poetry?

And the very first person
to ask to buy my book

A Cowboy

 Ain't that something!

I was feeling quite full of myself at this point. But we know there
are always two sides to every coin. I had always attempted to be
the man I hoped the world would see. So one day, as I was prepar-
ing to go out for the day, I was brushing my teeth clad in only my
undergarments, and this poem came to me as a bit of a humbling.

Ain't that Something

I strove to be
All that I could be
A man who said yes
When he meant yes
A man who said no
When he meant no

I tried to be
By my history
One who was kind
Walking the line
Showing no fear
Protecting those
he held dear

I tried to be
Forgiving and free
A man who was strong
Ashamed to be wrong
A man who knew pride
On the honorable side

Between you and me
There are secrets you see
My beautiful wife
The love of my life
I think on a dare
Bought me orange underwear!

Here, in a humbling sort of way, I wish to acknowledge this
gift that I possess, though sometimes it seems like a curse, isn't
something that I undertook by myself. Somewhere along the line,
someone planted the seeds of poetic life into my soul; I've merely
tended, cultivated, this gift from the Creator. I can't create poems.
Poems, words and phrases, out of nowhere attack my brain, and
I merely assemble the words into an order that befits my tongue.
Like when dealing with my children. The eldest fled to Minnesota
for love. Which is a wonderful thing, save for his "love" is a Vikings

fan. I grew up on Lombardi time. Deep within the bowels of alcoholism during the 1960s, the Green Bay Packers were all that I could count on. But as I've discovered, things change.

Living on Indian Time

Here's to my old hero Vince,
Words of praise I will not mince
Into his life we caught a glimpse,
Of my hero—one called Vince.

Out of the east to Old Green Bay
Vincent came to show the way
Do things right or you'll not stay
When he said right he meant "my way."

So we won and won and won and won
Making dreams for my Daddy's son
Showed hard work it can be fun
An investment for "the long run."

But there are tears within this verse,
That in old age just grow worse
I can't flee with a rich man's purse
This thing that I call "Lombardi's curse!"

On Lombardi time I was raised
Fifteen minutes early all my days
My sons, my daughters, my wife unfazed
A virtue, I thought: "I should be praised!"

Now I sit way past my prime
Contemplating hills I may have climbed
Standing alone in this driveway of mine
Raised a family with no concept of time.

Nails must be polished, for each and every date
Good things come to those who wait
Here I am, always late
Indian time, this Indian's fate.

A phrase started in my mind after hearing about the smallest room in the Vikings' stadium, the Super Bowl trophy room. To this I added the fact that while I was jogging one day, a dog came running out to chase me. The poor dog didn't realize a human being could run so slow. Just as he got to me, he had to put the brakes on. His toenails must have been too long, as I heard them scraping across the pavement. He couldn't stop in time, and he took my legs right out from under me. Scared the heck out of both of us. He never chased me again. However, I've encountered many dogs in my line of work that "will never bite." Yet I've been bitten twice. So I wrote:

Big Black Dog

Big Black Dog your teeth look sharp
Big Black Dog like an Asian carp
Big Black Dog sends a chill down my spine
Big Black Dog almost every time.

Working on the road
Trying to earn my pay
dueling traffic

each and every day
When a big black dog with teeth so white
Who the owner said "will never bite."
I'd heard it before as my blood ran cold
And my dreams of pain were taking hold.

He was stalking, to and fro
licking his chops 'cause I would know
That when I turned my back I feared
that stupid dog thinks he's thinning the herd
instinctively taking out the lame
Put an old man out, out of his pain

It's not that I have the greatest pride
As I hear his paws and his toenails slide
Across the asphalt out of control
I fall like a Viking at the Super Bowl

This surely ain't clean poetry
This ain't no glorious prose
I was a' lying with that Big Black Dog
Lying there nose to nose

I guess I was wrong
the owner was right
I'm half dead
But the dog didn't bite

He took off running
Scared out of his wits
do I look,
do I smell,
like bacon bits?

Poems and stories can magically appear. My wife and I were giving blood one day, as is our custom, when the nurse politely asked a question about her child's behavior. Having six wonderful children as we do (we are blessed), the nurse thought that we could be of help.

Her four-year-old didn't want to stay in his bed at night because there was a dinosaur in his room. I thought she should deal with the dinosaur first. She said that there was no dinosaur. I asked how she knew that. She was taking blood from my arm and telling me how many people I was helping. I didn't see my blood helping anyone. Just because she can't see the dinosaur doesn't mean one isn't there. She invited my wife back to give blood again, and she didn't say anything to me. That afternoon this song came to me.

There's a Dinosaur in My Room

There's a Dinosaur in my room, Momma.
There's a Dinosaur in my room, Daddy.
There's a Dinosaur in my room, Momma,
What am I supposed to do?

I was sleeping last night on my pillow,
When a Dinosaur woke me up.
He said, "Hi, my name is Willow
And, I need a little water in your water cup."

There's a Dinosaur in my room, Momma.
There's a Dinosaur in my room, Daddy.
There's a Dinosaur in my room, Momma,
What am I supposed to do?

So I jumped out of bed right then and there
And I came rushing in to you.
If you go in my bedroom, try not to stare
'cause the Dinosaur is painted blue!

There's a Dinosaur in my room, Momma.
There's a Dinosaur in my room, Daddy.
There's a Dinosaur in my room, Momma,
What am I supposed to do?

Now a Dinosaur is big and a Dinosaur is strong
And he's laying right across my bed.
It looks like he'll be there all night long
Could I sleep with you in here instead?

There's a Dinosaur in my room, Momma.
There's a Dinosaur in my room, Daddy.
There's a Dinosaur in my room, Momma,
What am I supposed to do?

Now my Momma told me not to be afraid
And she led me back to my door.
I said, "But Momma, I'm not afraid,
It's just that Willow snores!"

There's a Dinosaur in my room, Momma.
There's a Dinosaur in my room, Daddy.
There's a Dinosaur in my room, Momma,
AND HE'S GOT MY PILLOW, TOO!

My grandbabies all enjoy this sing-along song. Which then had to be translated into Grandma's fear of mice.

There's a Mouse in the House

There's a mouse in the house, our Momma screamed.
There's a mouse in the house, or so it seems,
The world is coming to an end.
There's a mouse in the house, my friend.

This morning I came wide awake
When Momma started a small earthquake
The roof flew off, the walls fell down
When Momma made that horrible sound.
It sounded like a mighty blast
More piercing than a whale's laugh.

When Momma turned on the kitchen light
And screamed as her hair stood up in fright.

There's a mouse in the house, our Momma screamed.
There's a mouse in the house, or so it seems,
The world is coming to an end,
There's a mouse in the house, my friend.

Daddy came a' running fast.
Me, I kinda shuffled in last,
Afraid to see what I might see
As Momma screamed hysterically.
She was standing on a kitchen chair
With both hands waving in the air.
She said he scampered right across here
He's under the stove, don't go near.

There's a mouse in the house, our Momma screamed.
There's a mouse in the house, or so it seems,
The world is coming to an end,
There's a mouse in the house, my friend.

Daddy grabbed the kitchen broom
And silently stole across the room
Then down on the floor upon his knees
Whispering, I hope I don't see it please.
Even though it was just a mouse
Like a knight in armor he was saving his spouse.
With his arm underneath the stove he squirmed
And wiggled like a giant worm.

There's a mouse in the house, our Momma screamed.
There's a mouse in the house, or so it seems,
The world is coming to an end,
There's a mouse in the house, my friend.

Daddy pulled out lots of stuff,
A great big pile of gray lint dust
He laughed and said to his stricken spouse
Honey, there's no mouse in the house.
So I went to look underneath my bed
To see if my new best friend Fred
Was sitting where he sits each night
Do you think a mouse as a pet is all right?

There's a mouse in the house, our Momma screamed
There's a mouse in the house and now it seems
I'll just hide him under my bed
And hope no one sees my best friend Fred.

Then we were lucky enough to have two beautiful children come into our lives, and I wrote this little ditty about growing up on a farm.

The Adventures of Sammy and Sam

An Adoption Poem

There once was a girl named Sam
And Sammy was her brother's name.
Now Samantha and Samuel they really were
But they liked Sam and Sammy just the same.
Now Sam had brown velvet skin
And she had black curly hair,
While Sammy was a handsome blond
But no one seemed to care.
Their Momma came from an Asian land
Their Daddy was an Eskimo
They all lived together on a little farm
They were a family, don't you know.
Now each and every morning
As the rooster called out the sun
They jumped out of bed and quickly dressed
And went out looking for fun
They went out looking for fun.

First they put on their coats and boots
Then they headed right out the door
If you're lucky enough to live on a farm
You have fun while doing chores.
They went to the chicken coop
Where under each hen they found

A whole bunch of eggs to take to the house
Some were white and some were brown.
In the shed Sam fed the kittens
And Sammy fed the dog
Then the rabbits and the calves
And the piglets, too, even the Mother hog.
They raced each other to the barn
Opened the door with a jerk
They laughed at the cows that had the horns
'Cause their horns didn't really work
No, their horns didn't really work.

Then their Dad gave them each a hug
And said, "Chores are done for the day."
Now, it's time for you to be a kid
Time to run and time to play.
So Sam and Sammy played
And they had fun all the day
But the best thing that they ever had
Were the hugs they got each day.
Mom and Dad hugged them every day.
And tomorrow it started all over.

A little bit of notoriety came my way from doing a number of readings around northeastern Wisconsin. I was even invited out to Clarion University in Pennsylvania to give a reading as part of the Martin Luther King Jr. speaker series.

With a bit of notoriety also comes a bit of responsibility. I was asked by some concerned citizens in Berlin, Wisconsin, to go to a school board meeting and give a talk concerning Indian mascots. I was allowed to speak for only five minutes. It takes me twenty

minutes to say hello! I was then asked to go down to Madison and testify at some hearing concerning the mascot issue, and naturally my pen began to write mascot poems.

I also became a bit disliked in Berlin. It was just at this time that my chapbook was coming out in print, and the paper seemed to be excited to do a story about my being published. We are a small town. Well, after I testified down in Madison, the local reporter wouldn't return my phone calls.

Indian, I Think

I'm an Indian, yes I am. I'm an Indian Man.
I'm an Indian, yes I am, I'm an Indian, I, I, I, think.

Born and raised on the reservation, corn soup in my veins.
Had Fry Bread at my graduation, but I think it kind of strange,
I don't look like what I see when you say you're honoring me.
I'm an Indian, yes I am. I'm an Indian Man.
I'm an Indian, yes I am, I'm an Indian, I, I, I, think.

I never saw my Mom or Dad dancing *woo, woo, woo.*
Grandma had no Tomahawk chop, she didn't have eyes of blue.
She never dressed in war paint, a little mascara now and then
She doesn't have a war lance or scalps hanging in her den.

Grandpa had one eagle feather, for going off to war
Now kids have full headdresses, bought at the discount store.
I never saw an Indian nose the size of a side of beef
And dental care on the reservation never gave us perfect teeth.

I never shot a buffalo,
I never speared a fish.
I don't cook dinner on a stick,

I use a fork and dish.
I never scalped a white man,
Or played bingo on TV.
Maybe I'm not an Indian,
So don't bother honoring me.

I read *News from Indian Country* and came up with this.

North Dakota Indian

Can't you see I'm honoring you,
'cause you are such a man
Can't you tell by looking at me,
my Grandma was an Indian
She don't have no feathers,
her eyes were pretty blue
The way she loves *Dances with Wolves*,
that's when we all knew

Grandma was a Braves fan,
she did the Tomahawk chop
She always loved the Hamm's bear,
and her beer she'd never drop
She said she saw old Sammy Baugh,
now he was a real redskin
Talking about American royalty,
Grandma was an Indian

I got a bow and arrow
when I was only ten
Smoked some dope, in the hope
to have a vision and then

Painted up my body
for a football game
Caught a cold or so I'm told
wearing a loincloth in the rain

Found some Polaroid pictures
of Grandma dressed like Cher
Long blond braids and halter top
with beaded underwear
Me, I do the boogaloo with feathers on my head
Your ancestors would say I'm honoring you
if only they weren't dead

Grandma was an Indian
An Indian princess
She had a princess phone
Glass moccasins

Then they shot Bin Laden.

Geronimo was an Arab

Geronimo was an Arab
Falling from the sky
Wounded Knee assassins
Call it battle when Injuns die
Football-playing redskins
Really have no clue
About 1653
And the bounty that we knew

Save a walleye
Spear a skin

It's the cowboys
Who always win
Save a walleye
Spear a skin
It's the same old song
Again and again

In baseball we got funny
Looking Indians on the wall
In college Chief Illini
Was dancing in the hall
Apples rolling down the road
Say they don't really care
As long as checks keep coming in
They'll be the first ones there

I hear the white kids singing
Hey, hey, hey, hey, hey
But it's not when the government
Is taking things away
The pain I feel is very real
And we all share the blame
For not respecting human beings
It's not some stupid game

Save a walleye
Spear a skin
It's the cowboys
Who always win
Save a walleye
Spear a skin
It's the same old song/Again and again

My mother and sisters were always treated with respect near my father and me. Dad had fists of steel. Me, I figured if I let them hit me in the head, they were bound to hurt themselves. Sadly, Dad and I were not always there. My wife and daughters have suffered, too.

Lies

It was fine in white society
For Momma to be a squaw
Tantalizing white boys' eyes
Each white boy that she saw
Black hair long and silky
Magnetic eyes of green
No one saw the human soul
Lost somewhere in between.

Andy Jackson shunned the law
Signed himself no truce
White society judged my race
Our morals were quite loose
Animals they called us bucks
Fate we couldn't escape
Women were just does in heat
They never called it rape.

Tom-toms beat in bleacher seats
Cheer our team to win
Half the crowd at any game
Says kill the Indian!

We all wanted to rock 'n' roll when we were younger. Me, I wanted to write songs like Tommy James, like Kris Kristofferson; I only

lacked talent. My children have talent thanks to my wife. One day the musicians in the family were out and about, and one guitar riff got my attention. I played that riff in my head and these words appeared.

Old Men Laugh

Old men laugh and young men cry
I want to live and I want to die
Riding these rivers made of stone
They're breaking my back and breaking my bones
Oh how you hurt me
Oh how you hurt me, Father
Crucified in Fantasy, Crucified in Fantasy

White men came in their black robes
Said they were going to lead us on home
Showed us the bible, showed us the way
Now we're living on this rez today
Oh how you hurt me
Oh how you hurt me, Father
Crucified in Fantasy, Crucified in Fantasy

The great debate rages on. Are race-based mascots harmful to the people who are being what many call "honored"? Study after study states the harm it does to our people, the Indians and our children. The big-nosed Indian in Cleveland, only Jimmy Durante could do honor to that Injun. The Tomahawk chop and chant in Atlanta, I've never seen or heard such goings-on here in Oneida. Then, the Redskins. White history books neglect to tell about the 1653 proclamation from the New England Trading Company putting out a

bounty on our people. To collect the money, all that was needed was a scalp with RED-SKIN attached to it. How many of us have bloodied our knuckles or had our bodies beaten because we were called "stupid redskins"?

The sad thing is, and the media makes it headline news, that many of our people do believe that we are being honored. Sadly, from my questioning, it comes down from our elders. Until I've explained what is really happening, the hurt and degradation that we suffer, many don't think that anything is wrong. It is truly lack of information and education that is hurting us. Remember, Sitting Bull was murdered by our own people, people who obviously didn't understand.

I wrote a song, an anti-mascot song, and should like to explain it.

Old men laugh

Now that I, too, am an elder, I can better empathize with "old men's" feelings that "some things just shouldn't bother us." Do we just accept this racism, this bigotry? When will it end? It has to matter; we have to stand together to fight this.

Young men cry

How many of us are still beaten down. How many of us still hear, "Indians get everything free." "More than three Indians off the reservation can still be shot." "Yes, you had the highest score but we hired someone else who will fit in better." How many of our children learn they are Indians by having another child sit on their chest, hitting them, and calling them a stupid Indian? Even one is too many!

Riding these rivers made of stone

There are still jobs, positions, and places not open to us. The river of equality is made of stone; we have to, and we need a pretty powerful force to, break through.

Breaking my back and breaking my bones

One day I was working in a confined space, dangerous work, and I asked our lead man if he had the proper training, first aid, etc. He assured me that he had, but that if anything happened to me, I'd be "just one more dead Indian." Without a witness, by law, people can say what they want, because who's going to believe an Indian?

Oh how you hurt me, oh how you hurt me, Father

How many times have our people been hurt? The Oneida were promised our ancestral lands by the Great White Father George Washington after we fought alongside him and his army, but our ancestral lands aren't really in Wisconsin.

Crucified in Fantasy

How often have we been crucified on the stage and screen? Perhaps even at school board meetings, public stadiums, "kill the Indians," and on the shores of lakes where we are fishing legally.

White men came in their black robes
Said they were going to lead us on home

The Jesuit priests came to convert our people. I was told that the gates of heaven were closed to those not baptized. It was a heavy load to carry for a third-grader to know that his Grandparents couldn't get to heaven.

Showed us the bible, showed us the way
Now we're living on this rez today

Becoming Christians didn't make our government treat us as Jesus had said we should treat our brothers. Maybe they should have led us instead of simply showing us how.

Only when we all go blind will we really come to understand. I am not a bear, a lion, or any other animal. I am an Indian; don't hang me on the wall like you would a trophy.

Things weren't always rosy on the reservation, either. I was attempting to be a part of the tribe by going to the meetings, writing for the *Oneida Times*, and being a part of the Oneida Arts program. At the meetings there is always discussion about different subjects, and some people have quite strong opinions. We are a matriarchal society and, as I stated before, I was raised by all sisters, so most of the discussion is from this side of the gender block. Having all sisters meant that I had to watch *American Bandstand* instead of *Spin an' Marty* after school. I also had to learn to dance, but a strange occurrence happens each time I dance—it rains. One time, my wife was attempting to teach me salsa dancing. I had to dance backwards for a whole afternoon, and then we had a two-week drought. My daughters suggested that I tap-dance,

but I said that I didn't want to drown. Anyway, I wrote about our Tribal Meetings.

Roberts Rules

My Daddy was a Catholic
They called my Momma squaw
The most interesting combination
That I ever saw
Bingo blood ran through my veins
Raging in my soul
Catholics found religion
Indians we found gold.

Robert's Rules of Order
Is what I always hear
When the clans all gather
And pow wow time is near
Robert's Rules of Order
Just make it go away
If we're a sovereign nation
How does Robert rule the day

We got the bingo parlor
We got the tobacco shop
Gifts handed down by ancients
That the government tries to stop
They sent us to the boarding schools
Gave cheese out as a ration
But Oneida stands on sacred ground
Call us a Sovereign Nation

I hold the sacred stories
Like treasures handed down
About the men of glory
Sacrificial blood upon the ground
They offered up their life, you see
So that we all could live
What greater love is shown to us
What more can heroes give

Tobacco has a sacred song
And bingo opened doors
But Robert's Rules of Order
Should be banished from our floors
We drove the British from our land
So let us show our youth
The turtle island is forever home
And Oneidas speak the truth

We know that money's a useful tool
But when our time is done
And when we make the journey
The Creator won't ask how much we won
As the Eagle flies above our land
It's our honor we will hold
And how we've loved our neighbors
I believe is what we're told.

Robert's Rules of Order
Is what I always hear
When the clans all gather
And pow wow time is near
Robert's Rules of Order

Just make it go away
If we're a sovereign nation
How does Robert rule the day

I also attempt to improve my craft. I go listen to other speakers and take classes when I can. I attended one class with a poet laureate, and his main emphasis during his talk was to never repeat a word or phrase more than three times. We were all supposed to bring a poem along to share, and, wouldn't you know it, he asked me to read first. I attempted to beg off, but here it is.

Old Man Fantasy

I was shocked, I was shocked, I was shocked, I was shocked
When it occurred to me
A car is a car is a car is a car
But some folks see things differently
Some folks see in the land of the free
Just a symbol of success
You don't go far in an Indian car
Described as a rolling mess.

I was fine for a long long time
Living in my little house dream
There was me and Ma
More kids than I saw
All the platters were all licked clean
Then one by one the children run
To feather their own little nest
There was I at fifty-five
Not ready to be put to rest.

So I went to school which was kind of cool
Had fun on my spring break
Then I joined the church and I ate perch
On Fridays instead of steak.
Now I write poems when I stay at home
Found that I had the time
Now I look they published a book
Full of my Indian rhyme.

I was shocked I was shocked I was shocked I was shocked
When it occurred to me
A car is a car is a car is a car
But a horse is fine with me!

I was lucky enough to have a horse when I was young. From television I thought that it was just natural.

My First Pony

My first pony
Was a loaner
My uncle
A big Indian
Loaned him to me
You might say
He was an Indian's pony

I was a cowboy
Actually
I was an Indian
A little Indian

Pretending
To be a cowboy
You might say
I was a loaner, too!

My horse's name was "Singing Wind." We called her "Windy." It was my favorite song.

Singing Wind

I was nine
She was nine
Tho more mature than I
Long black hair
That filly stare
Took me by surprise

I had a crush
A youthful rush
She kept me in my place
Came to find
Couldn't read her mind
By the look upon her face

A lady's whims
Her hidden grins
Mask passion in her soul
The queen of hearts
Right from the start
Held secrets I'll never know

We had a time
When we were nine
But the years just flew away
When spring is near
Her memory's dear
Brings a smile to my day

Whilst (I always wanted to use that word) I was down in Madison, our dear sweet governor Mr. Walker pretty much disbanded the Unions around here. I hope and pray that he did it for noble reasons, because if it wasn't for the Union, I would have never been able to advance in my career. My bosses now have deemed my crew quite competent, and we get many accolades from the tax-paying public. If all leaders were noble and honest, we wouldn't have a need for Unions.

Another reform that Mr. Walker instituted was insurance reform. This was a blow to my beautiful wife. Some of her beauty is earned by exercising, lifting weights, running, eating healthy, and applying lotions, notions, and potions of one sort or another all over her body (for which I am well grateful and the beneficiary thereof). But she ran into some difficulties concerning her French fry–eating, beer-drinking husband. We had to do health assessments.

Chips and Beer

In my years I've come to find, life is just a riddle.
Black and white make shades of grey, I'm somewhere in the
 middle.
I've accepted the fact, the love of my life, the one that I adore
Is totally concerned about my health,

My soul,
And so much more.

I recall our younger days, when life was just a riot,
Now she says she's getting fat, so she's putting ME on a diet.
Just this morning, at breakfast time, I found I wanted to scream
She told me,
We're lactose-free,
So no more coffee and cream.

The doctor all but raped my pride, poked me high and low
Vampires in white attacked my veins, then they let me go
The scale read, "One at a time," pharmaceuticals were my fate
The weight chart on the wall just read, you should be six foot
 eight.

Then my love, who's slight and trim, lifts weights and likes
 to run
Went to the doc, and to her shock, came back just looking
 glum.
She says that life is very cruel, the verdict shattered her day
Her numbers just didn't measure up, while mine were all
 straight As.

How can it be? She wondered out loud, through a gnashing
 of her teeth
Salads and fish her favorite dish, while all I want is beef.
French fries and eggs, I eat all the time, while she sheds a
 little tear,
Broccoli and corn, something I scorn, gimme chips and beer!

It didn't matter just how good my numbers were. She wanted to get me into shape. I said round is a shape.

Dieting with Debbie

I hurt, I hurt, I hurt, I hurt
From my head down to my toes
Exercising with my wife
My survival no one knows
We ride the bikes a hundred miles
Or so it really seems
We run, we jog, I sometimes crawl
To fulfill a young girl's dreams
There is no waste upon my waist
I've saved it for fifty-plus years
Who knew that in my golden age
I'd be paying for all those beers

She feeds me green, and red, and yellow
Even purple on my plate
Those aren't the colors of real food
A truth I'd like to state
Bread and gravy and French fries, too
Real food is brown
I look inside the refrigerator
That's one color never found
A tear rolls down my weathered face
As a carrot I press to my lips
Then a smile creeps upon my brow
Carrots and celery make swizzle sticks.

But once in a while, I come out on top.

Seeing Ain't Believing

You can tell the abundant love
That my wife has for me
As the days go rushing by us
Since I proposed on bended knee
She looks like a beauty queen
The wind blowing through her hair
Me, I look like Archie Bunker
Sitting in my living room chair
She enjoys her running
And exercising to a tape
With me along beside her
Planning my escape.

If I were to fall down now
With a heart attack to fake
There goes the cream in my coffee
There goes the chocolate cake
Perhaps a slight stress fracture
In my leg or somewhere else
But she'd say I'm too heavy
My chips would fall from the shelf
I wonder if I could convince her
I'm taller, yessiree
Where I used to touch the floor
I can only reach my knees
I guess that's not a good idea
For the cards that I've been dealt

She says to take a healthy breath
I might have to loosen my belt

Her love is on a deeper level
Of this I couldn't be surer
I caught a glimpse of my old self
Naked in the bathroom mirror
She still says that I am handsome
Which comes with a little twist
Just a little bribe inside the palm
Of her optometrist.

Then one day I was watching the food channel!

Diet-lishious

Stood on tiptoe
Ballet dancer
Drenched
In memories of food
Reaching
For the stars
Stole a piece
Of sunlight
Smiled it
Upon the world
Like Tony
Like Maria
The most
Beautiful sound
Painting pictures
Just once

Wanted to say
Green tea
Steamed shrimp
Dumplings

Then again, we now have twelve grandchildren.

Grandpa

Really
I thought to myself
Gliding down the highway
Pretty lady by my side

Feeling first date jitters
As I gently brush her hand
Knowing forty years ago
She agreed to be my bride

Tonight
We're on a mission
Secret agents on the prowl
From a '60s TV show

Carrying top-notch secrets
Grandma with a loving touch
Gift wrap shining bright
What's inside no one knows

But
Where pizza, beer, and chips
Meant party long ago
Each party turned into a riot

With silver in my beard
The spring in my step sprung
And a doctor's warning
Putting me on a diet

Well
Sometimes to be a man
We have to take a stand
Doing what we damn well please

It's my granddaughter's birthday
I love her very much
I'm a grown adult
I will eat macaroni and cheese.

It is hard to believe that I'm a grandfather. It is hard to keep up!

A Day with Grandpa

Run. Run. Run.
Grandpa, run.
Let's go to the park
And have some fun.

Run. Run. Run.
To the swing for a ride,
Run to the merry-go-round
Then to the slide.

Run. Run. Run.
Let's ride the bike
You on the big one
Me on my trike.

Run. Run. Run.
Let's play some ball
I'll hit a home run
You make the call.

Run. Run. Run.
To the ice cream store
We each get a scoop
Who could want more?

Run. Run. Run.
We run all day
Running is fun
And then I say.

Shh, shh, shh,
Don't make a peep
Grandpa's babysitting
Fast asleep.

V.

I AM TORN

 between
the wilderness of my youth
 and
the white world we call civilization

 between
the freedom of the fields
 and
the fight for human dignity

 between
the false comfort of an apathetic attitude
 and
the calamities inherent in having empathy
for my brothers and sisters of all nations

I AM TORN.

 between
the false security promoted by technologies
that leave us fat and swollen upon the couches
of our homes
 and
the savage need to rebel against an authority that fails to
abide by the very laws they are sworn to uphold

 between
the urge to close my eyes, to hide away from the injustices
of the world
 and
the desire to plant the seeds of freedom, of justice
to watch them bloom.

Please Lord, grant me the wisdom to overcome the conflicts
 of my humanity
 and
the courage to make my life meaningful.

Epilogue

Some things that I believe:

Thank the Lord for all his gifts, each day, in prayer.
Some gifts come in disguise.
Only boring people get bored.
Looks are a gift, beauty is earned.
Coaches should make ballplayers; parents should make men.
Hug your children each day.
Tuck your children in bed each night with open ears and a
 closed mouth.
Annoy your children with love.
Immigration problems may have started in 1492.
Tyrants want things done their way; leaders want things done
 the right way.
Take time to study clouds.
Fields of grain can really dance.
Miracles happen every day.
October is football season.
This is America; I will go where I want.
Children deserve to be forgiven.
We are all children.
Faith is a gift.
Take time to draw and color a picture.
Be just what you is and not what you is not; folks what do this
 are the happiest lot (Mr. Wizard).

Understand that you could be wrong, but make them prove it.

 You can teach a dog to fetch
 You can teach a dog to stay
 You can force a man to kneel
 You can force a man to pray
 You can lead a horse to water
 But you can't make him drink
 You can fill a man with knowledge
 But you can't make him think.

We are spirit and flesh; both need nourishment.

My family may call me an S.O.B., but I don't let anybody else.

If failure is inevitable, make it a memorable fight.

People who cheat to win, lose.

 Speak the truth
 It will amaze some
 Upset others
 Confound the idiots
 And ease your mind.

In the long run, people will give you what you expect of them, so expect their best.

At least once a year, gather children around you and eat popsicles until your brain freezes.

You can't take all the tricks without the Queen of Clubs.

If you don't win, act like you did, because you got to play.

Pro athletes are not heroes.

Hotels are not homes.

Read each day.

You can never run away.

Drinking four glasses of beer after a ten-mile run renders you almost invincible.

To get respect, give respect.

Give respect anyway.

Keep your bowels empty and your brain full.

People who straighten out their lives should be applauded.

People who've managed to keep their lives straight should be considered noble.

Work is a gift.

We are never alone.

Sometimes, take time to just enjoy breathing.

Listen to the silence.

There are ghosts.

There is nothing like a mother's love.

Toenails are not to be chewed.

When someone begins a sentence "I don't think," believe them.

The car fuel light is on for a reason.

You can't do it until you dream it.

Everybody knows something that you don't.

Don't expect others to help, but never hesitate to help others.

Never go down looking.

Never pitch low and away to a left-handed batter.

Winnie the Pooh knows.

Cry at the end of *Old Yeller*.

Seek nobility.

It is what you do when no one will know that defines you.

Get over it.

We are so soon old and so late smart, best we have one.
 (A sign in Dad's garage)

Always put your pants on standing up.

The same with your socks.

Being chosen last is still being chosen.

It is all right to be alone.

Acknowledgments

Thanks to Sister Mary Roberts and Sister Jean Patrice from St. Joseph Catholic School in Oneida.

And special thanks to Bruce Sanders from West De Pere High School, the best English teacher I ever had.

He said I could!

About the Author

Louis V. Clark III was born on the Oneida reservation in Wisconsin. Raised during the wonderful decade of the 1960s, Clark learned to stand up for what he thought was right, aided by the guiding hand of many influential people. He joined forces with his beautiful wife during their high school years, and they ran away to build their own life guided by the principle of "looking ahead seven generations." Now that his six children have graduated from college, Clark is focusing on his dream of sharing his experiences in the hopes of building a better world. Blessed with twelve grandchildren, he leans on his baseball background and says, "Never go down looking." This is his second book.